Ultralight Backpacking

The Essential Guide to Safe and Fun, Ultralight Backpacking for Beginners

BENJAMIN TIDEAS

ISBN: 1514784378
ISBN-13: 978-1514784372

CONTENTS

INTRODUCTION

Have you ever heard of ultralight backpacking? If you want to find out what it 's all about, this book is for you!

Ultralight backpacking is for people who want to experience the great outdoors without worrying too much about worldly possessions. It is for those who want to carry less yet still manage to care for themselves out there.

In this book, you will learn the essence of ultralight backpacking, how to assemble your ultralight backpack, how to set up a camp and how to keep safe with ultralight camping tips and strategies.

Backpacking becomes more fun once you learn how to be practical and resourceful. Get started on ultralight backpacking and experience true freedom now!

THE ESSENCE OF ULTRALIGHT BACKPACKING

Hello there, adventurer! So, you want to see the world? Well then, you should get acquainted with your closest companion throughout the journey: your backpack.

It is certainly not easy to carry your worldly possessions with you everywhere you go, which is why many seasoned travelers choose the ultralight backpacking approach. The essence of ultralight backpacking can definitely be found in its name. It kind of falls under the minimalist principle, which is to eliminate as much clutter as possible and to choose only the most essential items for you to keep with you.

There are plenty of benefits to ultralight backpacking. First of all, backpackers can get to more places at a faster pace because they do not have so much weight to carry. They also greatly reduce their chances of becoming injured during the trip. Many backpackers who carry a lot of weight on their shoulders for long periods of time have experienced back pain, shoulder cramps, neck aches and other discomforts that can otherwise be avoided with ultralight backpacking. Everyone can benefit from packing ultralight, especially those who plan to do long-distance trails from beginning to end.

In ultralight backpacking, only the most essential items are brought along, and anything that can be still be found in the place where the backpacker will be exploring does not have to be in the pack. It requires a thorough assessment of needs in comparison to the availability of these needs in the destination.

The ultralight backpacker must choose from among the top items that he or she has collected to place in the backpack without going beyond the weight limit. To save on both weight and space, an ultralight backpacker often chooses items that have multiple uses. Nowadays, there is a growing number of camping and trekking gear that are made to be especially light, compact, and multipurpose.

To understand the basics of ultralight backpacking, it is important to understand what base pack weight is first. The backpack and its interior and exterior gear is the base pack. The base pack does not include fuel, food, and liquid because these three are dependent on the type of travel and the duration. So, how much weight is there in ultralight backpacking?

In general, a true blue ultralight backpacker carries at most 9.1 kilograms or 20 pounds for long duration and 4.5 kilograms or 10 pounds of weight for a short duration. The conventional backpacker carries a weight that can range anywhere from 14 kilograms or 30 pounds to a whopping 27 kilograms or 60 pounds!

Ray Jardine, a highly experienced rock climber, was the one who made ultralight backpacking mainstream because of the books that he wrote about it. On record, he was able to finish his first Pacific Crest Trail with an 11-kilogram (25-pound) base pack weight and managed to get by with only 4.1 kilograms or 9 pounds of base pack weight on his third time to finish the trail.

Experienced travelers who apply ultralight backpacking recommend these guidelines to help first timers successfully pull off this approach:

Plan in detail. Visualize how you are going to get through the trip. What are the items that you will most desperately need? Which items can you source from the surroundings in your destination? It helps to visualize the entire trip so that you can pinpoint only the essentials. You certainly would not want to end up carrying a lot of weight that you do not actually get to use.

Choose items in their lightest and most compact design. Since weight is the priority here, you can let go of certain features and make sacrifices, such as having to pay more for the item or choosing the most lightweight but less durable ones. Just make sure that it will last you throughout the trip itself.

Weigh before you pack. You must have a pen, a paper, a calculator, and a weighing scale while you are packing. The first thing to do is to measure the base pack weight. After that, weigh all of the items you chose to take on your trip and take note of the weight of very one of them on a piece of paper before you put them in your bag. Once you have finished packing, total the amount of weight. If it goes beyond your target ultralight weight, then you will need to let go of some items. Also, be precise with your measurements.

Consider sharing gear. Two or more backpackers are definitely better than one because your group can divide the weight of certain items that can be shared, such as the tent, the stove, and so on. If this is your first time to take the ultralight backpacking approach, you might even want to consider borrowing the ultralight gear of someone else. This help you determine if you can commit to purchasing the items for another trip in the future.

Learn survival skills. Research, read, and apply the skills you learned from video tutorials and books. Skills such as how to start a fire, find a source of water, and create makeshift shelter are necessary not just for travelers, but for every human being who wants to stay alive during emergencies. Mastering these skills will definitely save you a lot of space and weight because you are confident enough to be resourceful along the way.

It might sound hard at first, but the truth is you will be able to survive with only the essentials. However, you must know everything you can about surviving with the basics. The knowledge and skills are necessary anyway, as what you want to do is to immerse yourself in the experience of backpacking without troubling over a huge and heavy backpack.

In the following chapter, you will find great suggestions on how you can pack light along with a checklist to make things easier for you.

THE ULTRALIGHT BIG THREE

In most backpacking cases, the items outside of the base pack that are brought along for the trip fall under 5 basic categories: food, water, cooking gear, shelter, clothing, and hygiene (including first aid supplies). In backpacker lingo, there is a group of items called the Big Three, and it consists of the backpack itself, the item for sleeping in (such as the popularly used sleeping back), and the shelter (such as the tent).

The weight of the big three are what you need to determine before anything else. However, you do have the option to purchase the backpack only after you have decided upon the number of items and have summed their weight. This can be a practical decision because you will find it easier to choose the best ultralight backpack that suits your needs.

Choosing an Ultralight Backpack

The base pack weight should definitely not be bulky. The bulk depends mostly on the frame, such as in internal frame packs that weigh close to 3 kilograms or 6 pounds. It is for this reason why some ultralight backpackers forego it. However, if you are not comfortable without a frame, you can choose a framed pack with the least amount of weight, such as choose one made out of silnylon, ropstop nylon, or Dyneema. On average, each weighs between 200 and 400 grams or 8 and 14 ounces.

When out shopping for an ultralight backpack, beginners would notice that all models are in liters. The recommended maximum capacity in liters for an ultralight backpacker is 65 for trips that can last for several days.

More experienced backpackers usually choose from a range of 40 to 50 liters. Find a design without additional unneeded features. While these packs do not have as many compartments to minimize weight, you can be resourceful in managing the items that you choose to store in it.

Keep in mind that there is a downside in choosing an extremely lightweight backpack as it is not as durable compare with those made with thicker and heavier material. Nevertheless, if you consider the lesser bulk that you will have to carry during your trip, then it will be worth it.

Picking a Sleep System

The combined weight of the sleeping pad and sleeping bag should be at most 3 pounds. Nowadays, this is a lot more achievable due to the high demand for ultralight gear.

Experienced ultralight backpackers usually purchase a 16-ounce sleeping pad and a 32-ounce sleeping bag for this to be possible. The material of the sleeping bag should be made of down instead of synthetic fills, as the former can be made more compact.

Backpacking in warm weather with a temperature of at least 40 degrees F will call for a simple hoodless sleeping bag or even just a quilt. A sleeping quilt is an insulated blanket but does not have insulation on the bottom, which makes the person depend on the sleeping pad for warmth. a hoodless sleeping bag also does not have insulation in its bottom fabric. The reason for this design is that the bottom insulation is nevertheless minimized due to the weight placed upon it. Ultralight backpackers who choose to scrimp on sleep system weight often set camp in areas that provide more protection against the elements, such as avoiding cold hollows, around thick vegetation, or next to cliffs and other natural wind barriers.

If you are planning to camp for 3 seasons then choose one that has a 20 degrees F rating. High-quality sleeping bags of this variety can cost an average of 350 US dollars. They can last for a decade, which makes them a good investment for those who plan to backpack frequently.

Choosing the Type of Shelter

There are now quite a number of tent options to choose from even if you are considering only the ultralight options. For 3 season trail backpackers, find a tent that weighs less than 2.5 pounds (40 ounces) and can be set up with hiking poles and not tent poles. These can be in the form of single-wall tents. Unless you are not alone during the travel, stick to the one-person design. A typical good quality tent with these features usually costs less than 300 US dollars.

If you are an experienced backpacker, you might even want to consider packing up a tarp or hammock instead since these are even more lightweight (from 4 to 16 ounces). However, they are not suitable for long duration trails since they are not as adaptable.

If chances of rain are moderate to high during your travel, then you most certainly need to consider rain shelter. Most tents that can adapt to rainy weather are quite durable but also heavy. They usually have two fabric layers to address internal condensation and are installed using stakes, metal poles, and even a ground cloth for the tent floor. For ultralight backpackers, you can minimize the bulk by choosing from the following options: a bivy and tarp combo, a hammock, a single layer tarp tent hybrid, a bivy sack, or a poncho tarp.

Review of the Big Three

Always make sure to make a canvas and total the weight of your backpack, sleep system, and shelter before you make any purchases. Aim for the minimal weight combination each time. A sample total weight range for the big three would range from 2.5 pounds (or almost 40 ounces) to 6.5 pounds (or over 100 ounces).

Once you have determined the weight and size of your big three, you can then use the remaining weight allowance for the rest of your gear.

ADDITIONAL GEAR

Ultralight backpack, sleep system and shelter? Check! The next step now would be to choose your gear. These are the footgear, the ten essentials system, and the survival kit.

The Foot Gear

The weight on your feet is a crucial number because it greatly influences the quality of your trip. Keep in mind the old saying: one pound on one's foot is five pounds on one's back. The heavier your shoes are, the more weight you need to lift with each step on top of your backpack. Ultralight backpackers make sure to minimize their footgear weight so that they can cover more ground, minimize energy (and consequently food and water) consumption, and reduce aches and pains.

The choice of footwear greatly depends on the terrain of your area as well as the type of trip. In general, it is best to opt for hiking shoes or even trail runners instead of hiking boots. If you do prefer to use trail runners, find a good quality pair that weighs about 10 ounces for each shoe. The typical hiking boot, on the other hand (or foot, for that matter), weighs about 35 ounces for each boot! The advantage to wearing hiking boots, however, is the ankle support that they give, but ultralight backpackers believe this to be a minimal gain for its weight.

Keep in mind that while lightweight shoes are not as durable, they are will still last for several years. The typical trail runner shoes can cover about 800 kilometers, and many popular seasoned backpackers have actually covered a wide variety of terrain, from mountain ranges to deep winter ones, while using them. They even go so far as to recommend non-waterproof trail runners because these dry faster and are much lighter.

Regarding the issue of shoes not being waterproof enough, consider the testimony of experienced backpackers who say that there is no such thing. Backpackers should accept the fact that their feet are going to get wet, which makes non-waterproof trail runners more advantageous in reality. The key is simply to give your feet, shoes, and socks time to rest and dry, respectively, after a particularly wet experience.

Socks should be thin and lightweight as well since a pair of these will not hold as much water yet maintain foot warmth and some cushion. You can even pack a pair of waterproof socks to slip on if you are about to go through water or rain. Just make sure to take them off during non-wet situations because they can be uncomfortable.

Aside from trail runners, you can also pack a pair of ultralight sandals for the kinder weather. Flip-flops are as lightweight as a pair of footwear can get, so go ahead and bring them along for the trip.

THE TEN ESSENTIAL SYSTEMS

Back in the 1930s, an organization in Seattle called The Mountaineers created a list of 10 essential items that outdoor hobbyists need to have for survival. It was not until 2003 when they changed the list of items into a list of systems. Each of these 10 essential systems contains a list of items.

It is important for you as an ultralight backpacker to find compact and multipurpose items that comply with the 10 essential systems. This is the list:

Navigation

During long trips, you cannot really rely on a digital map and compass because you do not know when the next time you can recharge your batteries will come. Maps are especially necessary for traversing off the beaten path, literally and figuratively. You need to learn how to read a map effectively before you go on your trip. A small guidebook or route description is super lightweight, so they are not a problem to ultralight backpackers.

The compass is also lightweight and independent from electrical power. Choose a small compass that has a sighting mirror you can use as an emergency signal tool.

Three season backpackers should also consider bringing a lightweight altimeter along because it can help determine air pressure and an estimate of the elevation. Such information is necessary to aid you in identifying where you are on your map.

Sun Protection

Pack up sunscreen lotions in sachets or stored in tightly sealed plastic bags. Bring just enough to last you until you can get to a store to re-stock your supplies. Find a good formula that can block UVA and UVB rays and with an SPF range of at least 15. This includes an SPF lip balm.

Backpackers should always carry a pair of sunglasses, especially if you are certain to travel across a terrain without shade. Choose a super light and compact one that can block 100 percent of UVA and UVB light. For those who will be following an ice or snow trail, pack up a pair of extra-dark glacier glasses. Bringing a wide-brimmed hat will also give you adequate sun protection.

Always wear your sunglasses throughout the trip and reapply sunscreen every 2 hours or more, if it is in the middle of the day and if you are perspiring heavily.

Clothing

Ultralight backpackers can go easy on the clothes but, depending on the type of trip, you need to choose these few pieces of clothing very carefully. You should also keep with you a few extra pieces of underwear and socks that dry quickly.

To help in choosing what to pack, think about the climate on the date of your travel. What kind of clothing will you desperately need during the days when you come across the season's most extreme conditions? For instance, if your trip is going to be during sunny weather, wear synthetic clothing designed to be lightweight and has Ultraviolet Protection Factor or UPF. If you are going on a winter backpacking adventure, you will need more clothes to keep yourself insulated. You can dress in layers, but make sure that these do not restrict blood flow because this will only counteract your plan to stay warm.

Learn how to fold your clothes in the most space-saving way to help keep things organized inside your backpack and save you space at the same time.

Source of Light

The most popular illumination option among ultralight backpackers is the headlamp, mainly because it is hands-free, quite light, and with batteries that last for a long time. Do not hesitate to bring spare batteries with you.

You can also choose to pack compact flashlights because their beams are quite strong and can also be used as an emergency signal during nighttime. However, it would be a better idea to find a good headlamp with a light beam that is adjustable so that you will only have to bring one illumination source with you.

First Aid and Hygiene

An ultralight backpacker needs to create a customized first-aid kit filled with multipurpose supplies to give room for items that are more suitable to his or her personal health needs. Consider how long the trip will last to determine how much of the first aid supplies you should bring with you.

In general, the first aid kit should contain a disinfecting ointment, blister ointment, gauze pads and adhesive tape. A pair of tweezers is lightweight and quite useful for blisters and getting rid of any stings and crawly insects. Over-the-counter medication for stomach problems, pain, and allergic reactions should also be considered. Find a container that will fit all of the items in a compressed way instead of a large kit that will eat up a lot of space in the backpack.

Do not neglect dental care during your backpacking trip as well. Always carry a small, travel size toothbrush and a small tube of toothpaste. A travel sized pack of dental floss will weigh close to nothing but will be incredibly helpful. Bathing might be a luxury during some days because of possible water scarcity, nevertheless bring along a small piece of soap (ideally environment-friendly), sanitizer gel, and/or wet wipes. Hands should always be cleaned before preparing food and drink. In lieu of a full bath, rub your face and armpits with clean water. Store all of your hygiene products in a resealable plastic bag or a small net pouch.

Fire Source

It would be wise for an ultralight backpacker to bring waterproof matches and place them in a waterproof case. Aside from that, a mechanical lighter should also be brought along. Both do not weigh much but are incredibly helpful to provide warmth and for cooking. Some backpackers like to keep dry tinder, chipped wood doused in resin, dried lint, or a priming paste in a zip-lock bag to help start a fire more easily.

If you are not sure whether you will be able to set up a campfire whenever you need to during the trip, then pack up an ultralight alcohol stove and a considerable amount of alcohol in methanol, ethanol, or isopropyl alcohol as fuel.

Repair Kit

The most useful and versatile tool for any backpacker would definitely be a knife. It helps create and repair tools, prepare food, and can all sorts of other emergency needs. Invest in a durable knife that has the following minimum features: flathead screwdriver, foldout scissors, and foldout blade. The less experience you have with backpacking, the more features you might need a knife.

Another must-have for any backpacker is duct tape. This tool is arguably the handiest thing to have in any emergency situation. It can be used to repair punctured water containers, fix trekking poles, seal wounds, and a host of other uses. Research as much as you can on how to maximize the duct tape before your trip.

Nourishment

The amount of food that should be brought along always depends on the type of trip. For ultralight backpackers, the choice of food for the trip should barely weigh anything, can be stored for long periods of time, and should no longer require cooking. Your body type is also an important factor to consider when packing the amount of food that you really need.

The minimum number of food calories that the body needs to stay alive is about 1,000 per 100 pounds of body weight every 24 hours. The more energy you expend, the more calories you need. The food should also contain low amounts of salt so that minimal hydration is necessary after the meal. Some suggested foods would be high-quality energy bars, jerky meats, nuts, dried fruit, and dehydrated food.

Dehydrated food can be bought or prepared at home. The typical way to re-hydrate the food would be to place them in hot water. Ultralight backpackers prefer to place the dehydrated food in a container of water. While this would require more time, it will spare you from having to carry a stove. Rolled oats and barley are some examples of foods that do well with this method.

Experienced ultralight backpackers advise that for thru-hiking, you pack approximately 1.1 kilograms or 2.5 pounds of food. For those who are planning a three season hike, you are advised to pack 0.57 kilograms or 1.25 pounds of food for each day. Choose foods that contain high amounts of calories for minimum weight, such as foods rich in healthy fats (fat is 9 kcal per gram while carbohydrates and protein are 4 kcal per gram each).

Store your food in animal-resistant containers, if possible. While these can add approximately 1.4 kilograms to your backpack, they will protect your food supplies from bears and such.

Water

Ultralight backpackers usually carry a collapsible water reservoir and a minimum of one 2 liter bottle of drinking water (about 2 kilograms or 4.4 pounds). It is imperative that you bring along items that will enable you to filter and purify water. Try to find a light disinfectant that can prevent waterborne diseases.

Before the start of the trip, highlight the areas on your map which can be reliable sources of water. Make it a habit to replenish your water supply throughout the trip, particularly before you move on towards a less predictable trail.

Emergency Shelter

Aside from the shelter that you would prepare for the Big Three, it would be a good idea to have an emergency space blanket or a durable trash bag that you can use to protect yourself.

Your resourcefulness, experience, and skills will help you figure out how to minimize the weight from the items that you have chosen to be your essentials. Adjustments can always be made based on your traveling plans. After you have prepared the essential items for your trip and found out that you have some weight and space allowance to spare, you might want to consider packing any of the following additional backpacker needs: a satellite telephone, a mobile phone, or two-way radios; a whistle, a PLB or personal locator beacon, and an insect repellent spray or lotion that contains picaridin or DEET.

It helps if you seek advice and tips from an experienced backpacker who has already completed a particular trail. He or she will be able to tell you the truly essential items that you need to pack as well as the skills that you should learn before you embark on your journey.

SETTING UP AN ULTRALIGHT CAMP

There are a lot of skills that you need to practice to perfection before you go backpacking, many of which cannot be contained within the limits of this book. However, some basic safety skills and strategies will be taught here.

Find a good campsite

If you are backpacking on a trail, the chance of you sleeping in a different location each night is high. It is for this reason that as an ultralight backpacker, building a campsite should require minimal time and energy. Seasoned backpackers do not even bring a tent along with them and would rather sleep under the sky. Newbies will not find this comforting and safe, however, so the next best thing to do is to practice setting up the tent that they have purchased at home. It is not a good idea to be setting up your tent for the first time during the trip as this will consume a lot of your time and energy. You will even want to drink more water than usual after such an endeavor and that is not good at all.

To find a good location for your camp, look for the flattest spot on the site. Experts recommend that you try lying on the ground first before pitching to check if the area is flat enough for sleeping on. You should also make sure that the place is not a hollow spot as rainwater will collect there. If it is going to be a particularly windy night, find a secure spot with a natural wind blocker. However, make sure that you are not close to any large trees with overhanging dead limbs. Avoid valley bottoms as these areas are usually the chilliest. If it is not too windy, try to find a spot that is uphill and camp there. Do not camp in the middle of an open field if it looks as if there will be a thunderstorm. While it might seem like a good idea to camp near a natural source of water, it is actually not advisable because you might deter the natural wildlife from access to hydration. For beginner backpackers, highlight the spots along the trail that are marked as campsites because these areas are tested and proven to be acceptable for settling in for the night.

After securing your location and pitching up your shelter, then next step would be to set up your camp kitchen so that you can prepare food and water.

Set up a Camp Kitchen

To set up your ultralight kitchen, find a large rock on which to place your cooking items, otherwise place them on the bare ground. Only light a campfire on a spot where you will not leave any damage. Never leave anything behind for the wild animals to eat. There have been numerous news reports on animals such as mule deer who suffered from starvation after having eaten plastic bags and other trash left behind by campers. Before turning in, secure your foodstuff in a bear-resistant container.

Otherwise, find a tree limb that hangs over 10 feet high. Place your food in a bag and tie it to the end of a long rope. Throw the bag and rope over the limb and secure the other end of the rope with a rock or some other heavy object. Keep the bag suspended at least 10 feet in the air to prevent bears and other wildlife from taking it.

If you are considering eating foods from the wild, the only recommended option is to go fishing. Foraging is generally not recommended because if backpackers get used to doing so, the area will be stripped bare and few or none will be left for the natural wildlife in that area. Streams and mountain lakes, on the other hand, are great sources of fish. You can pack a light fishing gear and the proper license if you wish to do so.

Once you have run out of water that you brought along for the trip, you need to find a good water source. The best way is to find a fast flowing stream or spring that is above bridges, trails, and campsites to collect water from. To collect water from a shallow puddle, use a mug or a jar and dip it into the puddle, then pour it into your container. If the source of water is too deep for you to crouch and collect, tie the end of a rope around the neck of a bottle and place a few stones inside the bottle. Lower the bottle to get some water. If the water source emits a thin trickle, use a piece of bark, stiff plastic, or foil to channel the water from the trickle into your container.

Keep in mind that just because the water is clear it does not mean it is potable. It could be teeming with life-threatening contaminants that will make your backpacking experience a living hell. Filtering is the first step to treating water so that you can get rid of as many solids as possible. You can filter it by pour it through a coffee filter or layers of clean cloth over the container. If your weight allowance has room for a pump water filter, you can use that as well.

After filtering, make sure to kill any dangerous organisms either by boiling or by using chemicals. Boiling requires a pot, so if you want to keep this as an option, choose the most lightweight small pot for you to tie to the back of your backpack. Create a makeshift stove by finding some large rocks around the campsite, then forming a circle that is large enough to hold your pot up. Inside the circle, create a small teepee of dry, dead firewood and place your firestarter inside it. Light it up and keep the fire steady before placing your pot full of water on top of the rocks.

While boiling is the safest route, it can be a difficult thing to do if you do not have the resources for a campfire. The alternative then would be to use iodine or chlorine tablets. Water treated either way will not taste very good, but it will beat dehydration and digestive issues.

Once you have a safe drinking water, you can start preparing and enjoying your meals for the night. It is always best to set up your camp before nightfall so that you can explore the area a bit to ensure security. Before preparing your food and drink, make sure to thoroughly clean your hands. Avoid sharing utensils with other campers to reduce the risk of contamination. Minimize the need for a cleanup by collecting any trash that you have and compressing them into a large resealable plastic bag for you to stash back into your backpack.

Set Up a Toilet System

An unavoidable issue while out backpacking in the wilderness is the toilet system. You can keep it simple and avoid having to bring so much toilet paper by carrying a lightweight camp trowel. To move your bowels, find a private spot that is not too far from your campsite (about 200 feet away from the cooking area and trials) and dig an 8-inch deep hole. Squat over the hole, do your business, wipe yourself clean, fill up the hole, and go back to the camp.

Materials that you can use to wipe yourself with aside from toilet paper is a clean rock (using the scrape method), sphagnum moss, woolly mullein, snow, or simply wash it off with some water from a bottle and using your hand (wash your hands thoroughly after the deed is done to prevent any health hazards later on).

The best type of soil to dig your hole is one that is dark and rich. Do not do your business anywhere near water sources.

Aside from the shelter, food, water, and a toilet system, another concern to address while setting a camp is to ensure the sanitation of your clothes. During long backpacking trips, it would be a good idea to find a large natural source of clean water so that you can wash your clothes and hang them out to dry before going on your merry way. Ultralight backpackers should be more vigilant with this task because they need to pack fewer clothes than usual.

ULTRALIGHT CAMPING SAFETY AND COMFORT

Practice makes perfect, so rehearse the survival skills that you have chosen to learn before your trip. Master how you can set up your tent because you will need this skill particularly during challenging weather conditions. Learn how to collect, filter, and treat water from natural sources as well as how to start a campfire. If you like, you can try sleeping in your sleeping bag a few nights before the trip to give your body time to adjust to the change. Before the trip, double-check your items to make sure that they are in working condition such as your stove and lamps.

It is important to learn basic first aid knowledge and skills. The best way to get the right knowledge and skills is to take a first aid course such as the one from YMCA or Red Cross. Bring a small, very light first aid handbook with you as a reference during your trip. Insect bites are a concern for backpackers, so choose to pack insect repellent clothing and a small spray bottle of insect repellent. Cover your ankles and wrists with cuffs as these are the areas that insects zero in on.

EMERGENCY TIPS AND SIGNALS

While out backpacking, make sure to turn off your mobile phone and other communication devices that require batteries because you need to conserve their power for emergency situations. Store them in a waterproof container so that they will not become useless in case you get soaked.

To send signals during emergencies, light and sound are your allies. Use your lamp or flashlight at any time of the day. A mirror can also be used to reflect sunlight and catch the attention of rescuers. Carry a plastic storm whistle as well. The common signal for emergencies in any situation would be six regular blasts or flashes, then a pause, followed by another set of six. During worst case scenarios, use your PLB to send out a signal via satellite and enable a search and rescue team to pick you up from the site.

To send an emergency signal to an aircraft, light a fire and then add wet vegetation to create a smoke. If possible create three fires that form a triangle; this is the commonly accepted distress signal. To use a mirror to signal an aircraft, let it reflect the sunlight against your palm, then flash the mirror upward and downward in the direction of the aircraft.

Safety should always be a priority when camping out. Even ultralight backpackers need to ensure that they have some sort of emergency tool in their pack before they embark. However, you should not let worry keep you from enjoying the great outdoors. Barely any ultralight backpackers ever experience getting themselves in emergency situations because they always plan ahead. They make sure to have the right skills and knowledge so as to have confidence in themselves. They are then able to enjoy nature and experience utter freedom by leaving their worries and excess baggage behind.

CONCLUSION

This book taught you how to prepare for an ultralight backpacking experience. It also included basic tips on how to start a camp and keep safe throughout the trip.

But do not stop here. Continue to learn survival skills and other tips and tricks. Aside from investing in the right gear for your backpacking experience, it is just as important to invest in yourself.

Finally, if you enjoyed this book, please click below to share your thoughts and post a positive review on Amazon. I would greatly appreciate your support!

Thank you and good luck!

Benjamin Tideas

ADDITIONAL RESOURCES

Please point your web browser to **www.plaid-enterprises.com** for more related resources, my full bibliography and to grab your FREE book!

Manufactured by Amazon.ca
Bolton, ON

16441690R00017